One Hundred Prayers
for
EVERYDAY PEOPLE

Jerry Patterson

Winston-Derek Publishers, Inc.
Pennywell Drive P.O. Box 90883
Nashville, TN 37209

© 1993 by Winston-Derek Publishers, Inc.

All rights reserved. No part of this book may be reproduced in any form without written permission from the publishers, except by a reviewer who may quote brief passages in a review to be printed in a newspaper or magazine.

First printing

PUBLISHED BY WINSTON-DEREK PUBLISHERS, INC.
Nashville, Tennessee 37205

Library of Congress Catalog Card No: 92-61370
ISBN: 1-55523-561-1

Printed in the United States of America

To the memory of my parents,
who taught me to pray as a child.

To the Reader

The following prayers are spontaneous expressions of faith, created in reaction to the uncertainties of daily living. If some of them relate to your needs or stimulate concern and meditation, then this little book has accomplished its purpose.

May God bless you always.

The Author

Prayer of a Husband

Dear God,

Make me a better husband and keep me ever mindful of what a wonderful Christian woman I have as a wife. Help me to control the criticisms, complaints, and occasional impatient reactions that seem all too common a part of domestic life. Let me show her each day in some particular way just how much I love her and how much she means to me. May all that I do add to her happiness. May I ever resist any temptation to be ungrateful as I would be lost without her.

May it be obvious to all who enter our house that our home is a Christian one and I pray that it always will be.

Prayer of a Wife

[Handwritten annotation: This goes out to my future Husband whomever He may be...]

Dear God,

    May I always be a good Christian wife and mother in your sight. May I support and encourage my husband in all his endeavors and be slow to criticize or find fault. Each day let me show him and our children what they truly mean to me.

    Guide me in creating a home that is based upon Christian teaching and conduct. Let me rear my children in an atmosphere of prayer, Bible reading, and dinner table discussion of issues involving Christian living, and may they follow the example of Jesus Christ all the days of their lives. Let me be constantly guided by the description of the good wife of Proverbs.

    May our home reflect love and Christian charity to all the outside world.

[Handwritten annotation: This goes out to all of my Strong Black Men and all Responsible Daddys...]

Prayer of an Alcoholic

Dear God,

It's hard for me to admit that I am an alcoholic, but I have no choice. It's even hard for me to get down on my knees and pray again, as it's been a long time since I last talked with you. Yet, I have to face the facts.

I have brought stress and mental anguish to my wife, my children, and even to my own parents. I am fortunate that my own life is not in an even worse condition, for I am a failed and miserable man.

Please help me, God, to break my dependence on liquor. Guide me in the therapy programs which I am now undertaking, and keep me away from those companions and situations which cause me to drink. Let me keep my home and family together and may my wife forgive me for the suffering I have brought to her. Forgive me for my sins and weakness of the past, dear Lord, and give me strength for the future.

Prayer of a Bigot

Dear God,

I admit that I am a prejudiced person and have been so most of my life. In fact, I developed these bigoted feelings so early in life that they have always seemed rather natural.

However, I realize that racial, religious, and national prejudice is inconsistent with Christianity and always has been—even in the days when the Church rationalized and condoned a certain amount of segregation. We cannot excuse ourselves of wrongful behavior just because of the traditions and customs of the society in which we are born.

Although I may not have personally or actively discriminated against others, I have passively done so and participated in the institutional prejudice of society. I have used racial slurs and told ethnic jokes and now I am aware how much damage those seemingly minor expressions can do. Attitudes and opinions are followed by action, and the influence of the spoken word is sometimes limitless.

Please help me, Lord, not only to eliminate my own prejudices, but to oppose bigotry as expressed by others as well. Change my attitude and make me a more tolerant and rational Christian and purge me of these immature feelings.

Prayer of a Materialist

Dear God,

Too much effort in my life has been spent on acquiring money, material possessions, and power, or what I perceived to be power. At first my goal was to gain wealth so that not only my family would have material benefits and security, but that I might also have money to give to the church and related charities.

In time, however, acquiring more money became an end in itself and I became less generous in my giving so that I might use present income as working capital for building an even bigger estate. Of course, I kept promising myself that eventually I would give more for God's work, but those intentions have not yet materialized. Even with an enviable net worth, I feel at this stage in life that I have accomplished little.

Help me, Lord, to change my priorities. I want to give more time and money to the Church and to related Christian activities. No longer do I want the acquisition of wealth and what it will bring to be paramount in my life. Direct me in putting first things first and show me where and how to channel myself and my possessions.

Prayer of One Who is Homeless

Dear God,

I am a homeless and unemployed person. It is not easy living in temporary shelters and from hand to mouth.

Help me to avoid being bitter or full of self-pity, and let me not blame others for my condition. I realize that I am mainly responsible for my being on the streets. Nevertheless, I ask for a certain amount of human assistance and generosity for those like myself. After all, Jesus expected the *haves* to show concern for the *have-nots*.

Above all, help me to break bad habits, make myself employable, and find a job whereby I may support myself, afford shelter, and contribute to a Christian society.

Prayer of a Woman Facing Surgery

Dear God,

Tomorrow I am to have surgery here in this hospital. It is a critical operation, and I must admit that I am afraid. Yet I know that I have the complete support of my family, my pastor, and above all, you, the Almighty.

Please direct the efforts of my surgeon, a Christian in whom I have great confidence. Calm and strengthen me through the operation and be with my family as they assemble at the hospital to be at my side. If it is your will, please grant me a complete recovery so that I may serve you in good health the rest of my life. Help me always to be a strong and steadfast Christian.

Prayer of a Job Applicant

Dear God,

I have several good job offers from which to choose. Please guide me in making a decision. Help me to honestly decide which of these opportunities will allow me to make the greatest contribution to a Christian society.

Don't let me be overly influenced by money, glamour, or location in making a decision. These considerations are valid ones, but will not solely provide job satisfaction in the long run. Help me to remember, in reaching our destination, we don't ask which road is the easiest or the most scenic, but which is the *right* road. May I choose the best path of employment; the one you want me to take.

Prayer of a Backslider

Dear God,

I have been the classic "backsliding" Christian. For many years I have had only nominal contact with the Church and have done nothing toward supporting it, nor helping promote its world mission. I now realize how much poorer spiritually I am as a result. My life would be in much better order had I been an active member of a congregation for the past twenty years.

Please help me in getting involved once again, God. Direct me to a church where I may find my proper niche and may contribute to its goals and mission. May I channel my energy and whatever talents you have given me in a direction that will allow me to make up for lost time. May I never again neglect the Church because of my own temporal involvements or my tendency to want to put the "things of this world" ahead of your designs.

Prayer of a Prison Inmate

Dear God,

   I am in jail and the fences and walls of this county prison aren't very encouraging as I try to think positive thoughts. The language of my fellow inmates in our barracks doesn't add much to the setting either.

   However, God, I know you are here beside me, and I know that you still love me despite the sin and crimes which I have committed. I am truly repentant for my misdeeds and my confinement here is not unjust. I promise that upon my release I will never do anything again that will return me to prison. Forgive me, God, and give me the strength necessary to grow as a Christian while imprisoned, and get me through this ordeal in the minimum time.

   I am thankful for the chapel and chaplain at this facility which provide comfort and encouragement for so many men. May we keep the faith we have worked so hard to cultivate here and keep our promises to You when we finally exit these walls. Bless the men here in this prison and I pray that every inmate may eventually find his way back to You. Help me to do my best in trying to exert a Christian influence on my fellow prisoners and by example encourage them to seek your divine guidance as well. You sometimes work in strange ways, Lord. Maybe that is why I am here just now.

Prayer of a Prison Chaplain

Dear God,

I am a chaplain in a county prison where I regularly counsel men who have committed crimes and are hurting inside. May I not think of them as criminals, but rather as unfortunate fellow sinners who have ended up behind bars.

Bless the families of these men who are confined, and may I do my part in keeping them in touch while separated. Let them be reunited in true Christian spirit upon the inmate's release.

May I do all I can to prepare these men for their return to society. Let me get them into active church membership and into rehabilitation programs as required. Let their newly-found, or restored faith be strong and sincere. It is easy for them to be contrite here in the confines of the prison chapel, but I fear the results of temptations to return to old ways and companions once they are outside the gates of this institution. Keep them steadfast, dear God, and help me to do my part in preparing them for their release day and in following up on their return to society. Finally, give me the resources to succeed, dear God.

Prayer of a Drug Abuser

Dear God,

I have been using drugs for the past few years. I knew that I was violating the law when I first began to buy and use this poison. I was curious about the so-called *thrills* or *pleasures* of the experience, and I was encouraged by friends who were users.

I have deprived my family of money that was squandered on this habit, and I now face the possibility of time in prison. I am presently seeking therapy to help kick the drug habit, but I know it will take stamina and hard work to succeed.

Please give me the strength to reform myself, dear Father. Bring me back to the Church once more and help me to remember that self-destructive pleasure means only pain in the long run. Help me to continually avoid any regression to drugs and any associates who would encourage me to use them again.

Prayer of an Egotist

Dear God,

I am aware that my life has been much too self-centered. Somewhere along the way I became too concerned with achievement, competitive accomplishment, and mass approval, and too little concerned with a Christian obligation to society. I have not shown nearly enough concern for my fellow human beings. I now realize that it is sheer futility and vanity to base my whole life on just myself.

Help me turn my life outward, Lord God, and apply my time, energy, and resources not for my own advancement and gratification, but for the promotion of the one thing that will last: your kingdom on earth. May I be more generous in giving to the Church and may all that I do for the rest of my life be directed toward making this world a more Christian one.

Prayer of a Parent

Dear God,

   Help me to be a better parent. I need to learn to be more patient and to remember that my children are not perfect and are not yet capable of behaving as mature adults. Let me learn to accept the fact that they will at times bring me disappointment and concern, not always pride and pleasure.

   Make me a better role model, Lord. Help me be more understanding, more flexible, and a better listener. Above all, help me to learn to control my temper and sudden spurts of anger which work against good parenting. I want my children to remember me as a Christian parent who helped them to become responsible Christian adults, and I pray that you will guide me in achieving this goal.

Rose, This is dedicated to my mom and Grandma

Prayer of a Daughter

Dear God,

I want to be a better daughter. It isn't always easy trying to care properly for an aged parent. Sometimes I feel frustrated in dealing with my mother and react in a rude or temperamental manner.

Give me more self control, God, and help me to remember the Biblical admonition toward honoring and loving one's parents. Help me to reflect back on all the many things my mother did for me during my childhood. I must have created many frustrating moments for her as well, and today it is only normal that our roles are reversed. May I always be concerned with my mother's happiness and be a better Christian in my relationship with her.

Prayer for the Terminally Ill

Dear God,

I have a terminal illness and I confess that the prospect of dying is fearful to me. I have tried to live a Christian life, but I'm not sure just how successful I've been. I have made compromises throughout life and have committed acts for which I fear judgement.

However, I find comfort in the scriptures and the promise of divine forgiveness. Please forgive me of my sins for which I am truly regretful. Help me to live an exemplary Christian life in the time I have remaining. I only wish that I had my life to live over. I'm sure I could be a much better Christian.

Comfort my family. I thank you for their continuing support during my illness. Give me courage and awareness of the love of Jesus Christ during these coming months.

Prayer of an Unwed Pregnant Teen-ager

Dear God,

I am a teen-ager who is unmarried and pregnant. I am concerned about the future, but I know you will hear me as I pray.

I was considering an abortion, but you heard my prayer and forbade me to take the life of my own child. Now I look forward to having my baby. I will rear this child to be a Christian and provide for it to the best of my ability. However, any other children I have will be born in wedlock and will be fathered by a loving husband.

Forgive me for my wrongful acts and for the unhappiness I brought to my own parents, dear Lord. Make me a good Christian mother and provide a good life for my child.

Prayer of a Ministerial Candidate

Dear God,

I am aspiring to become a minister of my church. Please help me to appreciate the serious obligation which goes with my candidacy. Help me with my own self-evaluation in determining if I have the necessary qualities and commitment for this life I am choosing. If so, then let me not ignore the call for a single moment longer.

I want to serve you all of my life, dear Lord. Please grant me the necessary endorsements that will allow me to enter seminary and eventually become ordained. Let me not be discouraged along the way, and may I constantly be guided by our saviour, Jesus Christ, as my role model, not only in my quest for the ministry, but through all the days of my life.

Prayer of a Missionary Candidate

Dear God,

I have just completed the initial testing and interviewing for mission service in my church. I am eager to serve as I want to play a role in the expansion of our church's foreign missions. Yet, I have some reservations. I have not spent any real time outside of the United States, and, as a single woman, I know how much I will miss my family back home. I have often heard it said that few people are truly qualified to serve as Christian missionaries.

Please, God, let me know if I have the necessary inner resources and support which I will need to serve you in this capacity. If not, then direct me toward another means by which I may better serve you and my church. I know you will be with me in whatever decision I make. Strengthen my faith and my ability to serve.

Prayer of a Widow

Dear God,

My husband has been dead for one month now. I have adjusted to the initial shock, but I am afraid it will take some time to deal with my feelings of loneliness.

Yet, dear God, I know there are consolations and compensations. I am blessed with a Christian family and friends for emotional and spiritual support, and they will always be available to me. Also, my lack of responsibilities will allow me more time for church and charitable work. May I involve myself as quickly and completely as possible and gain the satisfaction that comes from serving you.

Protect me from self pity and show me where and how I may best serve you, Lord God.

Prayer of an Adulterer

Dear God,

I am a man who has been unfaithful to my marriage partner and have committed adultery. I love my wife and always will, but I was tempted by a beautiful and personable woman who is a co-worker. I know that I was sinning when I first began this affair, but I expected it to be a brief encounter. It has now gone on for almost a year.

My paramour is a divorced woman and I believe she would like to marry me. Please guide me and give me the strength to end this affair immediately. I don't want my own marriage ruined, and I hope she can soon find a new marriage partner and establish a Christian home.

Forgive me for the commission of this sin, God. I feel very guilty. Give me the maturity and strength to resist any such future temptations. Make me a better man, husband, father, and above all, a more steadfast Christian.

Prayer of an Angry Man

Dear God,

I lost my temper again today and said things that I regret. It seems that when I am angry I forget all about being a Christian, and I justify my reaction towards the person or situation that brought on my burst of anger.

Lord, I must learn to try harder and restrain my anger. It is especially regretful when I become angry with a member of my own family. Help me to realize that I often behave like a fool when I lose my temper, and that an angry man is "full of poison." I am hurting myself physically and emotionally when I allow my anger to take charge. Let me in the future be "slow to wrath," so slow that I will stop to pray when I feel my temper beginning to rise. Please give me the patience and stamina to overcome this fault.

Prayer of the Unemployed

Dear God,

    I lost my job just a few days ago. Not only am I now deprived of money with which to support my family, but am also suffering the feelings of lowered self esteem and respect, which come with unemployment.

    God, please guide me in finding work which meets with your approval. Let me present myself to prospective employers as a willing Christian worker who believes in giving an honest day's work for a fair day's pay. Don't let me be tempted to take any job that would be unsuitable for a Christian. Finally, watch over my family during this difficult time, and aid me in acting quickly and resourcefully.

Prayer of a Christian Friend

Dear God,

It's hard to realize just what a blessing friends are. Possibly the older we get, the more we appreciate them.

I thank you for all those people I call friends. My best friend has devoted much of his life to the Church and is a "doer, not just hearer" when it comes to Christianity. I pray that I may always be as good a friend to him and all the others as they have been to me. Let me continue to expand my circle of friendship, God. Finally, may I have an exemplary Christian influence on each of them.

Prayer of a Soldier

Dear God,

I am a member of the armed forces of my country. I joined the Army for the purpose of protecting and defending my nation, but I pray that I will never have to wage war nor take human life in accomplishing this mission. May my actions as a soldier always be in deterring war and aggression and not in creating it.

However, if and when I should be called into combat, may it be solely for the purpose of securing national or international peace or to protect the lives of fellow human beings. May I never fight in a war which is motivated by material greed, or power, cloaked under the name of *"national interest."*

Even under combat conditions, may I exercise Christian conduct toward the enemy and charitable concern for all noncombatants within the war zone.

Keep me active in the Church, dear Lord, and in close contact with my chaplain wherever my assignment takes me.

Prayer of a Lawyer

Dear God,

I pray that you will always help me be guided by Christian principles in the practice of my profession. May I remember that I became a lawyer because I wanted to promote justice and legal reform in society, not just because I hoped to make a lot of money.

Make me ever aware that I am an officer of the court and have the obligation to see that honesty and justice prevail. Please don't let my zeal for my own client or my desire to win in court cause me to do anything that is unethical or dishonest or unfair to any concerned. May I remember to also give my time and income to charity and to the Church. May I set a good Christian example for my clients.

Prayer of a Doctor

Dear God,

Please help me in my goal to sustain and improve human life. May I always be more interested in the welfare of my patients than in becoming wealthy.

Above all, may I remember that I am only an instrument in your hand when it comes to healing and saving human life, and may I never be guilty of trying to reverse our roles in my own mind. May I always be a source of courage and inspiration to my patients. Let them think of me not as simply a good doctor, but a good Christian doctor, who cares about their souls as well as their bodies.

Prayer of a Sunday School Teacher

Dear God,

It is a real privilege for me to begin today teaching a Sunday School class for junior high students in my church. I believe that Sunday School teachers contribute almost as much toward Christian growth in the church as does the minister.

Let me realize, oh Lord, just how great are my responsibilities and opportunities. My preparation and presentation of the scripture lessons can either lead a young teen-ager to an active life as a Christian, or alienate him from the church permanently. My appearance and personality are important too, as I want to be a role model for my students.

Be with me, God, as I attend to this task. Give me the enthusiasm, knowledge, and techniques to succeed. In the years to come, may I realize the joy that comes from seeing Christian men and women in whose spiritual development I played a part.

Prayer of a Minister

Dear God,

I thank you for the ability you gave me to become a minister. My work is never done, but I would not exchange my job for any other in the world.

I love the responsibility of shepherding my flock and the small part that I play in the Church's world-wide attempt to establish God's kingdom here on earth. Yet, there are disappointments also. Diminishing membership and lukewarm participation can be discouraging. Divisiveness within the congregation takes its toll as well, and sometimes my schedule leaves me at the point of physical and emotional exhaustion.

Yet, you always seem to give me added strength, Lord. Please continue to do so. My work, or should I say *our* work, affects all eternity.

Prayer of a Traveler

Dear God,

I am about to embark on a journey throughout a number of Third World countries, where I expect to see some novel and unique sights. However, I want this trip to be more than just self-indulgent sightseeing.

Most of the people I will encounter are not Christians. I hope to have a good cultural exchange with them and, although I am not traveling as a missionary, I need to be a model Christian. I pray that some day these people or their descendants will know Jesus Christ as their personal savior. It is our responsibility to make it happen.

Please watch over my health and safety as I travel, Lord God. May I show myself a Christian to all with whom I come in contact.

Prayer of an Actor

Dear God,

I am in a profession which is not closely associated with the Church or Christianity. It is true that many actors' private lives are notoriously linked with un-Christian behavior.

I admit that it is not easy to work as an actor and be a good Christian as well. The film and television industries are controlled and influenced by people who are not Christians. Their productions often feature violence, sex, and life styles in conflict with Christianity.

Yet, I can turn down any part in a production which is morally objectionable. I have never done a beer or cigarette commercial, nor worked in a film I considered immoral.

Finally, the Christian actor has many opportunities to influence his coworkers toward the life of Christ. He or she may have even more opportunity as a Christian role model for young people. May I never find it necessary to turn down an invitation to visit a church congregation or youth group, and may I always use my talents for the glory of God and Jesus Christ and never for Satan.

Prayer of a Gambler

Dear God,

I am a gambler. I'm not really a professional gambler who earns his entire living by games of chance, but the appeal of the practice seems to be growing on me.

For years I gambled just a bit for the fun of it. Now I'm spending more time and energy at the gambling tables and my losses are increasing. Gambling fever is getting a hold on me.

Help me, God, to break this evil habit. I realize that only a fool would throw away his money in this manner. Help me to remember the evil and crime associated with organized gambling and how every casino I've ever visited has been truly the devil's playground. Also, help me to remember the financial disaster that gambling has brought to so many homes. Help me to break the habit, God, and think constantly of my family and my obligation to them and to you.

Prayer of a Policeman

Dear God,

All day long I deal with anti-Christian behavior and am constantly exposed to violent and irresponsible people. Even many of my fellow officers value physical power and toughness more than they do the traditional Christian virtues. I often suspect that some of them even see me as a *goody goody*, rather than a tough, intimidating cop.

Yet, I feel that a good policeman must be a good Christian. May my bearing on duty always reflect a good role model. May I never use force against any person unless it is necessary for the protection of others or my own self defense. May I never overreact and use physical force punitively or vindictively. I became a policeman to protect and serve my fellow citizens. Make me ever mindful of that obligation, dear God.

Prayer of a Football Coach

Dear God,

I teach boys to play a game that is based upon physical ability and power, not Christian charity or humility. Yet, I believe I can have an influence on my players and help them to mature into good Christians.

Let me never confuse game aggressiveness with the desire to injure or inflict pain upon an opponent. Help me to control my temper at all times and even more important my language during practice.

May my criticisms be constructive and designed to build up each boy's self esteem, not reduce it. May I emphasize good physical conditioning and proper care of the body, which is our temple here on earth.

May our prayers before each game be sincere and thoughtful and influence each man as he enters the field. May my own personal conduct and religious life within the community have a good influence on my players. May each be a better Christian man for having played football for me.

Prayer of a Professional Athlete

Dear God,

As a professional athlete, I am nationally known and my life and career are observed by many sports fans, especially the young. May I always be a good Christian role model and exert a positive force on anyone who might admire me or be influenced by me, both on and off the playing field.

Help me to conduct myself as a Christian during competition and exercise good judgment concerning my associates and activities in my private life. May I never be tempted to endorse or advertise any product which could lead to un-Christian behavior. Protect me physically during competition and keep me from injuring any of my opponents. May I always play according to the Golden Rule.

Prayer of a Teacher

Dear God,

I am a teacher in the public schools. I want to teach Christian values as well as necessary skills and knowledge to my charges.

May all that I do within or without the classroom be proper conduct for a Christian. I realize that I must not violate the First Amendment to the Constitution in teaching religion in the classroom, but there are still many ways to direct the student toward Christian behavior without violating the law. May all who enter my classroom feel a Christian atmosphere and know that I am a follower of Jesus Christ, and may I work tirelessly to do the best job possible for my students and the public who employ me.

Prayer of a State Legislator

Dear God,

I am a member of the legislature of my state. I am thankful that my fellow voters elected me to this position and are thus giving me the opportunity to represent them. May I always serve them as a Christian.

May my vote never be influenced by favors or gifts or venial interests that would make me less than objective. May I vote only for those bills and measures which will promote a Christian society within my state. Even if this policy means taking an unpopular stand and jeopardizing my chances for re-election; help me to stick to it, dear Lord. Bless my fellow lawmakers and may we serve Christ as we serve our State.

Prayer of an Artist

Dear God,

I am attempting to earn my living as a painter. I hope to create work that will add to the beauty of the world. Much of my work will be religious art which I hope will convey the spiritual truths and statements which I want to establish. Ecclesiastical art has influenced our civilization for the past thousand years and may it continue to do so.

May I never use whatever talent you have given me to create immoral or anti-Christian works of art. May I always use my influence as an artist to discourage the public exhibition of such productions.

Guide my hand and eye so that you and I are creating together.

Prayer of an Office Worker

Dear God,

I am a clerical worker in the head office of a national corporation. I like my job. My employer is a socially responsible business, and our chief executive officer is an active Christian.

May I always be a good, loyal employee who gives her best to the job and speaks well of her employer and co-workers. Help me to avoid the temptation to engage in gossip or vulgar stories or other wasteful activity with my fellow workers. Let them feel that they can always rely on me when they need a supportive friend, or a sympathetic listener. May my conduct be such that I will always be recognized as a Christian.

Should my company's policies ever go against my Christian beliefs, give me the courage to seek another job immediately. I want my career to play a role, however small, in bringing about your kingdom on earth.

Prayer of a Factory Worker

Dear God,

I am a worker on an assembly line in an automobile plant. The work is monotonous, but we produce a good product and I have good wages and job security.

I am thankful for my job and the support it gives my family. May we always produce a safe product that will protect the lives of those who use it, and may I always be conscious of my responsibility to do my job thoroughly and carefully.

Much talking goes on while we are at work on the assembly line. Without appearing as a prude, let me avoid laughing at or encouraging the dirty stories and vulgar comments that are so common among us—especially those that degrade women and minorities. Keep my mind on better things, dear Lord, as I earn my daily bread.

Prayer of an Employer

Dear God,

I am the owner of a small business. May my goals as a business person always be consistent with the doctrines of my church and may they make our community a better place in which to live.

May I operate my business not only for profit, but also to provide necessary goods and services to my community and to provide satisfying jobs for my employees. May I never be dishonest in any business transaction nor greedy in dealing with my customers or employees. Finally, may I be fair and considerate of my competitors and adhere to the Golden Rule at all times.

Prayer of a Retiree

Dear God,

Last month I retired from my job and now have a great deal of time on my hands. I pray that you will bless my retirement with good health and may it be a time of joy for both me and my family.

Now that I have much leisure time, dear Lord, please help me to use it properly. May I not devote my days simply to the golf course, or a comfortable chair in front of the television set. Let me use my time constructively and in service to you. Open to me volunteer opportunities within the church or church-related activities, where I may truly serve the Master. I am certain that the more actively I serve you and my fellow human beings, the healthier and happier my retirement will be.

Prayer of a Writer

Dear God,

I am a professional writer which means that I have absolute control of when I work and what I produce. I have been financially successful in my work, but now I am seeking a truer and more lasting success.

As you are already aware, I have written some novels of which I am not proud. They were published and were fairly successful on the market, but I don't feel good about them today. They pandered to the reader's interest in sex and they featured characters who got what they wanted in life by following an aggressive, less than Christian, code of conduct. I wrote those books out of greed, knowing that they would be popular and make money for me.

Please help me, God, never again to be tempted to write that kind of material. Let the works which I produce in the future be devoted to promoting Christian living and values. May all who read my stories be encouraged to live the kind of life which Jesus Christ advocated.

Prayer of a Social Worker

Dear God,

I am a social worker. My work is sometimes depressing as I deal with what most people think of as the misfits of society.

Please give me the energy and the stamina to deal with this stressful job. Don't let me give in to the discouragement that besets so many of those whom I try to help. May I not only bring tangible benefits to the unfortunate, but let me also live so that I set a Christian example for them. Finally, may those to whom I minister receive more concern and generosity from society in general, especially from those of us who consider ourselves Christians.

Prayer of a Farmer

Dear God,

As a farmer, I make my living working closely with You and rely a great deal on nature for my success in life. The past few years have not all been good ones for farmers, and friends of mine have sold their land and moved on to other endeavors.

Yet, you have been good to me, God, and I want to continue producing food for my fellow human beings. Don't let me be guilty of asking for too much. I can't always expect you to let it rain just for my benefit. I can't expect the grain market, the bankers, or support from government programs to always react according to my needs. Help me to remember that a good farmer is self-reliant and trusts you to do the rest. May my efforts and my land always produce and add to your bounty on earth.

Prayer of a Stock Broker

Dear God,

I am engaged in a business which is often associated with power and greed. My customers expect me to make money for them and some are frankly greedy and materialistic people.

Yet, I feel there is nothing wrong with the accumulation of wealth. It can be used to bring financial security to a family and it can be donated to the advancement of Christian purposes. Let me not be guilty of greed myself. May I never encourage a client to assume more risk with his or her money than he or she can afford, just to make more money for myself. May I never suggest a purchase simply because it means a larger commission for me. May I follow the legal and ethical regulations of the business to the letter. Finally, may I always be thankful for the good income you provide for me and my family and may we be ever generous in our Christian giving and remember God's commission first.

Prayer of a Merchant

Dear God,

I am a merchant in a small town. I thank you for the success of my business and the comfortable living it affords my family and me.

May the consumer goods which I sell in my store contribute to both the spiritual and physical well being of my customers. Last year I discontinued selling tobacco products in the store, although these items carry a high profit margin. Please don't let me be tempted to ever stock them again. Also, let me constantly monitor the books and magazines left on our newsstand to assure that I am not selling literature that will serve the devil. May I always offer quality goods at a fair price to those who bring me their business. Thank you for my customers and my loyal employees. May they always know me as a Christian businessman.

Prayer of a Television Producer

Dear God,

I am a television producer. I work in a highly competitive and power-oriented industry where survival means success.

I must please both networks and sponsors in order to survive myself. Many with whom I deal are not Christians, and it is often hard to stick with my own values. Help me, God, to remember why I entered this business in the first place. I wanted to provide wholesome entertainment that would be suitable for all members of the family and would promote Christian attitudes and values. If I find that I can no longer produce that kind of program successfully, then let me find another occupation rather than compromise my standards. I am bothered by the violence, poor taste, and advocacy of anti-Christian life styles that are currently portrayed on our television channels. Let me do all within my power to counter this trend.

Prayer of a Reformed Hunter

Dear God,

I have been hunting for sport since I was a teen-ager. I admit that I have never killed game that did not provide food for someone, including on a few occasions children in Africa who otherwise would have had very little protein in their diets.

However, traditional arguments notwithstanding, I have recently convinced myself that slaughtering animals for the sport of it is wanton disregard for their right to live and not too far removed, in essence, from murder. I once felt that there was something very strong and masculine about stalking big game with a high-powered weapon in my hand, but now those feelings seem immature. I promise to hunt for sport no more, God. Please help me keep my vow.

Prayer of a Nursing Home Occupant

Dear God,

I have recently moved into a nursing home. It is a bit hard for me to adjust to this new environment having lived for so long in my own home.

I know you will help me make the necessary adjustment, Lord, and I don't want to start feeling sorry for myself. After all, none of the other people in this home came here out of complete freedom of choice, either. You've never failed to hear my prayers before, and I know you aren't going to forget about me now. Let me be a model Christian and friend to the others in this home. Some seem so lonely and unhappy. Let me concentrate on brightening up their lives. Keep me active, but please don't let my family and friends forget that I am here.

Prayer of a Smoker

Dear God,

I am not only a cigarette smoker, but a heavy cigarette smoker who has been at this habit since youth. It is time for me to quit, so please give me the strength and self-discipline necessary to do so.

I realize that each time I light up one of these little white devils I am slowly committing suicide. It is sinful to abuse one's body and jeopardize one's life. I am not only wronging myself, God, but my family as well. My life and my family mean much more to me than a self destructive pleasure. Let me break the smoking habit, dear Lord, before the habit destroys me.

Prayer of a Parent of a Retarded Child

Dear God,

We have just learned that our child is badly retarded. I was not prepared for this news and it has come as a severe shock.

Yet, may we always love and appreciate this child as much as we would any other. May all of our decisions regarding his upbringing be based upon what is best for him. May we rear him to become a Christian and, despite his handicap, may he effectively serve you. May we avoid any sense of self pity or tendency to unconsciously blame this child for the condition over which he had no choice. Finally, may we be thankful for the challenge you have given us as Christian parents and with your help do the best job possible in rearing our son.

Prayer of a Teen-ager

Dear God,

I am a teen-ager and in a period of life which many see as experimental and rebellious. I admit that I frequently disagree with my parents and often feel they are just plain wrong on certain matters. Yet, help me to realize that they have more experience and maturity, and have shown so much love in trying to create for me the best life possible.

I want to become a good Christian adult, Lord. Help me to do so. I am often tempted to do certain things for the thrill of it, or to impress my friends. Help me to resist these temptations and avoid becoming involved with those who will get me into trouble. Furthermore, make me a good influence on my friends who may be weak.

Thank you for my family and my church. May I always follow the life of Jesus Christ as my role model.

Prayer of an Automobile Driver

Dear God,

Every day I drive an automobile to and from work and for my own recreation and pleasure during other times of the week.

My car is a great convenience to me. It is also a potential weapon of death. May I always drive carefully, defensively, and with Christian concern for all others on the road. Let me avoid driving when I am tired, irritable, or when I have drunk any alcoholic beverage. Let me impose upon myself a fitness standard that would be appropriate for the pilot of a commercial flight any time I get behind the wheel. To drive with any less self-discipline is to show wanton disregard for the lives and safety of all society, and can set a poor example for teen-age drivers. Make me an exemplary driver, dear God, and a stronger Christian day by day.

Prayer for a Homosexual Bar

Dear God,

Across the street is an establishment known as a gay bar. It is a place where homosexual men meet and make contact with one another.

As Christians, we cannot possibly condone sexual acts between members of the same sex. Neither can we ignore these men in their quest for love and companionship. In the spirit of Jesus who would not have condemned them, let us welcome them into his church and try to get their hearts and minds turned in the right direction.

These gay men will have to resolve the changes in their own lifestyle themselves, but we can help. Let all who call ourselves Christians support them and pray for them. May the church provide counseling, psychiatric assistance, or whatever it may take to reconcile their lives with you, dear Lord. Give us the strength and will to make it happen.

Prayer for an Adult Book Store

Dear God,

I just exited the adult book store behind me on the street corner. It is adult only in the sense that it excludes anyone apparently under the age of eighteen years. Actually, it caters to a very juvenile and prurient sexual orientation.

Yet, I must admit that while thumbing through the magazines I saw some pictures that were very appealing. I also saw disgusting examples of art and photography and some features designed to appeal solely to perverted tastes.

Lord, in the future, keep me out of this sort of shop. I don't want this kind of art to influence my desire for sex. Maybe censorship isn't the answer, but help us change the tastes of society at least to the degree that pornography is no longer big business and no longer so easily available in any large city within our nation. We have so many sex crimes. Let the church take a stand to stop the flow of this sort of poison before the adult book stores become our urban schools for sex education.

Prayer for Sympathy

Dear God,

A close friend's son has been killed in an automobile accident. I am on the way to see him now and I want to prepare my expressions of sympathy.

Please don't let me speak in trite, banal terms, which though well intended may fail to convey any real expressions of sympathy. Instead, help me to remind him of the many happy memories which he has of his son over the past twenty years. Let me recall his son's achievements and his justifiable pride not only in those accomplishments, but in his own fine record as a father. May my words be candid, to the point, and brief. Help me to remember that too much company during a time of grief can be fatiguing and that a short visit is more comforting than a long one.

Give my friend strength, God, and may he always be aware that his son is now with you and that I am available when he needs me.

Prayer for the Golden Rule

Dear God,

How I wish that I could always follow the Golden Rule. It seems simple enough as it is only an eleven word commandment which is completely compatible with human nature. Why do I have so much trouble consistently following it?

I can provide my own answer. We often rationalize situations and see things from our own point of view instead of objectively. Our pride and ego and maybe even our prejudices get involved and we believe that we deserve somewhat better treatment than the other person. Sometimes even a little cheating on our own behalf seems acceptable.

Let me avoid these pitfalls in my own life, God. Let me stop and measure every action I take by the Golden Rule and let me do it honestly and objectively. Otherwise, I cannot be a real Christian and a true follower of Jesus Christ.

Prayer for World Peace

Dear God,

World peace is an enigma. All nations and peoples claim to favor it, but few governments will forego the use of force when their own national interests are threatened.

Wise men have concluded that a state of war, not a state of peace, is man's natural condition. It does seem a bit too easy to motivate people to take up arms. War can be easily glamorized.

May the Church then make every effort to change human nature and to counter the Jingoism that seems inherent in so many of us. Televised coverage of combat operations helps show the destruction and suffering of war. May all the world have access to this grim presentation and may it serve as a deterrent toward further violent wars. Fear may be our only deterrent until it can be replaced by love.

Prayer for the Economy

(handwritten annotation: OUR worldily People ourselves...)

Dear God,

Bless our economy and give us national prosperity. Help us to control inflation and to increase our national and per capita incomes as well.

We do not ask for this blessing because we are greedy, but because many are unemployed and others are still not earning sufficient income. Also, so much good can come from wealth used generously and properly channeled through the Church. Our hospitals, orphanages, and universities attest to that fact.

May we always be thankful to you for the prosperity you have already given our nation and be ever generous in our tithes and gifts as we seek to establish your kingdom here on earth.

Rose

Prayer for Decision Making

Dear God,

I find it increasingly difficult to make decisions. I am developing a tendency to postpone dealing with important issues rather than meeting them directly.

Help me to rely more on you, dear Lord, and less upon my own human resources in deciding matters. May I bring decisions to you in prayer and let you show me which course I should take. Help me to consider all facts clearly and not be motivated by lack of commitment or selfishness. Don't let me be misled by rationalizing or thinking that the easiest, or most pleasant course of action is right.

Once you and I reach the decision together, Lord, give me the strength and the guidance to act upon it and never lose faith.

Prayer for Cheerfulness

Dear God,

Help me to be a more cheerful person. We make ourselves happier and make the world a more pleasant place when we spread a bit of cheer.

Let me never miss the opportunity to pass on a pleasant greeting or a compliment to friend and stranger alike. Let me be aware of the many chances I have to make people feel better about themselves. This is the essence of the Golden Rule. However, let me avoid the temptation to amuse others with vulgar language, ribald stories, or ethnic jokes. These are means of cheap popularity and do not spread cheer nor good will in the long run. May my attitude always be on the positive side, not the negative.

Prayer Concerning Anxiety

Dear God,

Why is there so much anxiety in my life? It seems that I am constantly anxious over my health, my finances, and the future.

First let me get my priorities straight, Lord, and decide just what is worth worrying over and what is not. Next, let me seek expert advice on matters which are unclear to me. There are good Christian doctors, lawyers, and financial advisers readily available. Finally, the Bible reminds us that you are always watching over us and are a constant source of comfort and strength. What more security do I need?

Prayer for Sensitivity

Dear God,

Help me to show greater sensitivity to others. It is so easy to overlook their feelings when I am caught up in my own concerns.

Let me develop the habit of showing more gratitude and appreciation for the favors shown to me. Help me to look for opportunities to pass on sincere praise that will please and encourage another person. Help me to remember names so I can convey to others the fact that I recognize them as distinct individuals and that they are important to me. On the other hand, let me never be guilty of unthinking comments that would offend or embarrass another person. Gossip, jokes, and ethnic slurs may all cause ill feelings unintended by the speaker. The lack of intent does not make the pain less real. Let me practice each day the skills of being a better listener and observer of others so as to know better their feelings and needs. Finally, may I show more sensitivity in my own communication.

Prayer Concerning Arrogance

Dear God,

Protect me from the temptation to be arrogant. I am often guilty of arrogance without even being aware of the fact.

Sometimes I am a snob and at other times I let my pride influence my attitude toward others. I know this behavior is contrary to Christian virtues. It may seem natural to judge other people by our own standards and values, but help me to remember that all people are equal in your eyes and the stereotypes that so many of us have in our own minds were created by society and not by you, the Almighty God. Finally, let me remember that arrogance is completely contrary to the teachings of Jesus Christ.

Prayer of Thanks for Nature's Beauty

Dear God,

How often do we remember to thank you for all the natural beauty of this planet and universe? I admit that I seldom remember to do so.

Yet, look what a constant source of visual and physical pleasure you have given us in nature. Its charms are accessible to all the peoples of the world with only a minimum effort. Quite simply, the best things in life are free. I never feel quite so close to you, God, as when I'm gliding along a river in the middle of a rain forest or looking down at a chain of mountains from an airplane above.

Let us always take care of this planet you have given us and strive as Christians to preserve its beauty and vitality.

Prayer of Thanks for Created Beauty

Dear God,

We thank you for all works of art which men and women have created throughout the centuries and for giving them the necessary talent and skill to produce them. We further thank you for the fact that so much ancient art is preserved today for our enlightenment and enjoyment.

Let these objects of beauty encourage our talented contemporaries of today. May creative genius always be inspired by you, dear Lord, and not by Satan. May the talented among us not waste their abilities on work that will encourage sexual lust or prurient interest, or will pander to vulgar tastes.

Instead, may every artist be a missionary whose creative efforts will be blessed and acceptable in your sight.

Prayer Concerning Compromise

Dear God,

Protect us from the sin we condone when we compromise with evil. We usually feel that we are being tolerant when we are actually being weak.

We allow pornography to be published and distributed under the guise of freedom of speech and then must deal with the poison it spreads throughout our society. We call homosexual practice an "alternate life style" and then watch that life style lead to moral and physical self destruction. Some churches are even willing to compromise by condoning certain expressions of sex outside of marriage.

Lord, may we remember that moral codes and commandments are not the result of current opinion polls, and contemporary society does not determine what conduct is or isn't a sin. Jesus Christ did not compromise with evil and may we have the will to follow his example.

Prayer for Generosity

Dear God,

Make me a more generous Christian. I want to give unselfishly, but it seems that there are always so many priorities demanding my money before I get around to paying out your share.

It is often more difficult to be generous with time than with money. We know that we should give you the first fruits, but it is easy to get so absorbed in earning a living, rearing a family, providing ourselves with the recreation we feel that we deserve, that we have precious few hours to devote to your work.

Let me organize both my budget and schedule so that you will never be short-changed. I know that there are Christian activities that will provide me as much recreational value as my present forms, and with far more satisfaction. Also, I spend more money on non-essential luxuries than I should. I need only think of the prosperity you have given me in order to divert some of the luxury money to the church, and to my less fortunate fellow human beings. Let me no longer ignore my obligation to God and the Church.

Prayer Concerning Lying

Dear God,

How hard it is not to tell lies from time to time. We know that lying violates the Ten Commandments, but we often do it almost unconsciously. Even our national leaders are sometimes less than completely truthful.

We lie to save face, to protect ourselves from blame, to cover for an error, and even to amuse and entertain. Yet, even the so-called *"white lies"* are a perversion of the truth and they are habit-forming.

Some of us start out telling innocent lies, but they become so habitual that finally we have difficulty in separating the truth from fantasy. Most of us are familiar with the unfortunate pathological liar, who has lost all self control.

Help me to remember, God, that lying is an immature habit. A true Christian will always tell the truth and accept the consequences. May I always remember and adhere to that standard and give no person reason to ever doubt my word.

Prayer for the Sabbath

Dear God,

Keeping the Sabbath holy is not so easy today as it was several generations ago. In modern America, it is a day of commercial activity for much of the population.

Help us to concentrate on what is meant by *holy*. Certainly you expect us to spend a portion of the day in organized worship. The remainder of the day is well spent in constructive reading or in outdoor recreation, but let us strive to make the recreation the sort in which the entire family may participate. A family picnic or volleyball game in a quiet natural setting seems more consistent with Sabbath recreation than does attending a commercial sports event.

Finally, help us resist the temptation to make the Sabbath a day for shopping. We have six other days of the week for that activity. May our Sabbath always be your Sabbath, oh Lord.

Prayer Concerning Duty

Dear God,

Duty and Honor were watchwords of the mid-Victorians who felt that these two virtues should determine one's conduct. The term *duty* is not used so much in that context today.

Yet, our Christian duty is just as real today as ever. We can discover plenty of examples of it if we look around us. Our paramount duties as Christians is to set a good example for others, care for our fellow humans, and bring the rest of the world to Christ.

It is certainly the duty of the strong to help the weak and the rich to help the poor in this world. Every relationship implies a Christian duty be it husband, wife, parent, child, sister, brother, friend, employer, employee, neighbor, pastor, and on and on. Open our eyes that we may see our duties clearly, Lord, and direct us in unhesitatingly performing them.

ROSE

Prayer Concerning Setting a Good Example

Dear God,

We all set examples for others. Unfortunately, they are not always good examples.

We all find ourselves guilty of hypocrisy from time to time. I know I have been guilty of setting bad examples for others both by word and deed. We do this when we are not thinking, angry, or failing to exercise self control.

Help me, Lord, to remember those who set both good and bad examples for me as a youth, and try to copy the former. Make us always aware of who is observing us and how much just one word or reaction might influence that other person.

Finally, may we always strive to follow the example of our only true role model and savior, Jesus Christ, and develop the habit of asking ourselves constantly, "What would He have done in this situation?"

Prayer for Health

Dear God,

Thank you for the blessing of good health. It is a gift that most of us too often take for granted. It is only truly appreciated when we no longer have it.

Please help us to remember that our physical well being is almost entirely in our own hands. We abuse our bodies not only in such obvious ways as through the use of drugs, alcohol, and tobacco, but also through passive ways such as failure to eat, rest, exercise properly, or follow a physician's advice.

Remind us, God, that our bodies are the temples you have given us to dwell in during this life and that these temples will serve us only as well as we serve them. Make us ever mindful of the Christian obligation to be healthy and in good physical condition.

Prayer for Home

Dear God,

May this house always be a Christian home. May the decor as well as the spirit of all who live within suggest to those who enter that the spirit of Jesus Christ can be found here.

May this house always be a place where prayers are said daily and the Bible is read regularly. May it be a place where all family members are loving and supportive of one another. May it never be the scene of angry quarrels, bitter accusations, or hostile behavior. May all who knock at the door of this house be received politely and kindly. If Jesus ever comes to visit us, may he immediately feel at home.

Prayer for Justice

Dear God,

Bless our efforts to maintain justice in this world. It is not even easy to agree upon a definition of the term. The wise, though pagan, philosophers Plato and Aristotle had difficulty.

Justice means that all people shall be treated equally before the law and by their fellow members of society. Yet, let us as Christians go a bit further and learn to temper justice with mercy. Help us to remember that consistency of criminal punishment, not harshness, is the leading deterrent of crime. Let us also remember the role that forgiveness plays in Christian living and incorporate it into our judicial system.

Prayer for Learning

Dear God,

Make us aware of the Christian obligation as well as privilege of learning. Let us also remember that our minds were not given to us just to use for our own pleasure and amusement.

May we remind ourselves that learning is not restricted to formal educational programs found only in schools and colleges, but may also be done right here at home in our easy chair.

It goes against your will when we let ourselves remain ignorant. May we read only the best of books and watch only the best of television programs, especially those which will encourage Christian living. Let us not fill our minds with junk entertainment any more than we would fill our stomachs with junk food. May we be knowledgeable Christians helping to create and maintain an informed and enlightened society.

Prayer for Work

Dear God,

Thank you for work and the meaning it gives to our lives. Despite all the complaints we hear about it, most people would lead lives of tedious boredom without work. It brings us income and self-fulfillment and it largely defines who we are.

Guide us, Lord, in choosing our life work and in selecting the right job. May our work be completely compatible with our Christian faith and may we perform it with the objective of establishing your kingdom on earth.

May we not be tempted to consider money alone in our vocations. Help us to remember that service to you and to our fellow man are more important. Also, protect us from becoming workaholics, and don't let us be so concerned with success that we forget the purpose of life. Let us remember that you are the ultimate employer of us all, and it is your "paycheck" that really matters in the end.

Prayer Concerning Temptation

Dear God,

Please give me more strength in resisting temptation. There are pleasures of the flesh that are hard to resist and it is so easy to rationalize acts which we know are motivated by selfishness and greed.

Lord, when I am tempted to sin help me imagine that Jesus is here beside me. How would I react as I looked at him? What would he say to me? Am I where I would be pleased to take him? Am I involved in the sort of activity of which he would approve? Help me to avoid idle time and people whom I recognize as a negative influence. Help me to stay out of Satan's territory and move along when I sense he is near. Finally, let me be ever aware of the power of prayer in combating the temptation to sin.

Prayer for Melancholia

Dear God,

These past few weeks I have been depressed. There are certain things in my life that I must change, but feel incapable of doing so. I am guilty of feeling a bit sorry for myself as well.

Renew my strength through my faith in Jesus Christ, oh Lord. Let me seek help in prayer and scripture and even in advice from Christian friends. Don't let me wallow in self pity, but let me face each problem and decision with the firm and positive approach of a Christian. Grant me energy and physical vitality to pull myself out of the doldrums, knowing that you are with me at all times.

Prayer Concerning Sexual Lust

Dear God,

Protect us from the attractions of sexual lust. The sex drive is strong in most of us and at times difficult to control.

Let us remember why this strong urge is given to us and help us to channel it into a Christian marriage. Deliver us from the temptations of extramarital and pre- marital sex and any aberrations into sexual deviance. May we not degrade ourselves with pornography. Remind us that sex is not a plaything created for pleasure alone, but a natural part of life designed for maintaining a happy marriage and for procreation of the human race.

Prayer Concerning Suicide

Dear God,

We pray for strength and guidance for those who are tempted to commit suicide. We do not want them to enter eternity with the crime of murder on their hands.

Help them to remember that the taking of human life, even one's own, is a terrible sin. We did not create our lives and we have no right to end them and cause unhappiness for other innocent people. Give the would-be suicides the courage to live out their lives and comply with your divine intention. Let them not be influenced by well-meaning groups or individuals who read self determination into the act of suicide, and help these people to realize the wrong they are doing in encouraging another person to commit murder.

Instead, let all Christians be aware of any signs among friends and acquaintances that might indicate a possible suicide attempt, so that we may provide help immediately. May we be aware of the necessity to preserve life, and to bring prayer and spiritual aid to those whose spirits are down.

Prayer for the Government

Dear God,

We pray for your blessings on our federal, state, and local governments. May those who are elected or appointed to office at all levels be guided by Christian beliefs and the Christian spirit in performance of their duties.

Protect our government from corruption and its leaders from greed and too much desire for personal power. May we elect Christian men and women to office so that those who serve will be accountable to you and to the teachings of Jesus Christ in formulating public leadership and establishing society's laws. May we, as voters, always be guided by our Christian beliefs as we cast our ballots.

Finally, may we support our government and those whom we have elected by active participation in political life. May we never cheat on our taxes, nor criticize government leaders without knowing the facts. May our nation never go to war except for self defense or for the protection of those victimized by an enemy aggressor.

Prayer Concerning National Pride

Dear God,

Protect us from an excess of national pride. Patriotism is an admirable trait so long as it doesn't encourage aggressive or chauvinistic attitudes towards other nations.

Above all, don't let our nationalism encourage us to feel superior to other nations. Extreme nationalism in the early twentieth century helped bring on two World Wars and suffering for millions. It has brought on numerous civil wars and insurrections. May our schools teach nationalism in a non-aggressive manner and may our churches encourage us to be Christians in a world society first and members of a particular nation second.

Prayer Concerning Language

Dear God,

Help us to control the use of vulgar language. It is far too common on our streets today and in the entertainment media as well.

Those who constantly swear or resort to obscene words and expressions show insensitivity toward others and obviously don't have Godly thoughts on their mind. Let us show them better ways of expression by our example. May film producers, authors, song writers, and performers become more responsible and avoid the liberal use of vulgarity in their productions. Make them aware of the negative influence of this sort of language, especially on the young who pick up the words and expressions from the media.

May the Church never shirk its role in opposing obscenity and pornography.

Prayer Concerning Pain

Dear God,

We ask your blessings and comfort for those who are in physical pain. Grant them strength, stamina, and hope in bearing their suffering.

We are thankful that medical science of the past few centuries has learned to control and reduce much pain. May our society always support these efforts. May those who presently suffer have reason to hope for a rapid improvement in their conditions, and may we encourage them in this regard. Help us, oh Lord, in our daily lives to exercise safety and caution in both work and play so that we may not bring on accidents that will cause injury and pain.

Prayer Concerning Pleasure

Dear God,

We are thankful for the technology of the twentieth century which has brought us comforts, conveniences, and pleasures never afforded previous generations. Yet, we ask that pursuit of ease and pleasure not become our primary reason for living.

Pleasure should be the dessert of our lives and not the main course. Yet, so many of us have become spoiled by the materialistic *"good life"* that we seem to see it as the real purpose of living. Turn our efforts toward happiness, not just pleasure, Lord. Let us know the joy that comes from following your commandments, living the Christian life, and serving our fellow man so that our pleasures in life are more meaningful.

Prayer Concerning Agnosticism

Dear God,

We pray for the agnostics of the world. May these often intelligent and well-educated people abandon their stubborn and unrealistic beliefs and accept the true state of God and his universe.

We earnestly importune these doubters to rely more upon faith and less upon tangible evidence. We must all measure ourselves by *your* standards, not measuring You by *our* standards. Help us to direct our agnostic friends to the reading of cosmological and ontological arguments of religious philosophers as well as the Holy Bible itself. Open their eyes and enlighten them, Lord. We don't want them to leave this life still rejecting your love and salvation.

Prayer for Repentance

Dear God,

Make us truly repentant for our sins. We knowingly and willingly commit these wrongful acts, seek forgiveness, and then often commit the same sins once more.

True repentance should be a deterrent toward such backsliding. Let us ask ourselves if we are truly committed to you. May we not be lukewarm, oh Lord, but remember that the "new self" we put on in Christ will free us from sin. I have made a commitment to You and am repentant. Give me the power to resist further sin and temptation.

Prayer Concerning Self Deception

Dear God,

Keep us from deceiving ourselves. We rationalize our actions arising from prejudice, greed, and selfishness as innocent expressions of self preservation and practicality.

May we realize that we cannot fool you, though we attempt to fool ourselves. Let us be honest about our own conduct and learn to ask the old question that is still as effective as ever, "What would Jesus have done?" When we get on our knees and clear our minds of our own self interest, the answer should be obvious.

Prayer Concerning Stress

Dear God,

Protect us from stress in our lives. It seems an inherent, even necessary, part of living, but let us learn to control its effect on us.

Help us learn to put matters in their proper perspective. If we attune ourselves to your will, few things will seem worth the anxiety of stress. Also, let us remember that being busy and being involved in constructive work or other activity will often make us less anxious and crowd worry out of our minds. Finally, let us utilize the relaxation and comfort which comes from prayer, especially if done at regular intervals throughout the day. With your help, oh Lord, stress need only bother us if we create it ourselves, or fail to take the right measures to control it.

Prayer Concerning Superstition

Dear God,

Keep us from the foolish, if not harmful, practice of allowing our lives to be influenced by non-Christian practitioners of the occult. Help us to remember that astrology, horoscopes, fortune telling, and similar expressions of pseudo-science are as useless today as they were when denounced by the prophet Isaiah over two thousand years ago. Some of those who purport to be witches and warlocks border on being tools of Satan.

Let us remember that we may adequately know the future through the inspiration of scripture and need not resort to the prating of frauds. Guide us to use our time and mental energy for the pursuit of true knowledge, not trivial superstition.

Prayer Concerning Communism

Dear God,

We give thanks that the Communist Party is losing power in Europe and other parts of the world. May the Church grow in strength and influence in these former iron curtain nations as the atheistic teachings of Marx and Lenin lose their hold on the people.

May we not only purge the world of Communism, oh Lord, but of the conditions that created and nurtured it for the past century and a half. We pray that Russia will once more become the Christian nation that it was for fifteen centuries. May we concentrate missionary efforts in the countries where Communist teachings have flourished, now that the time seems so appropriate. Bless the Christians and prospective Christians in these societies traditionally hostile toward all religion, and may they gain our undying support through both prayer and action.

Prayer for the Entertainment Industry

Dear God,

We pray for your healing of the entertainment industry. Here in the United States it is now very sick.

Please help our film and television producers, our book publishers, and our music industry to realize that success is not entirely dependent upon graphic exploitation of sex, obscenity, and violence. Films can still do well at the box office without satiating the dialogue with four-letter words. Television ratings can be high without series segments that publicize sexual deviancy. Music will sell without glorifying suicide. Christians must provide the medicine. May we support with our prayers and money those groups who are presently trying to purge the entertainment industry of the filth that saturates it. Let us work for better entertainment, or else we will be responsible for what we get.

Prayer for the Church

Dear God,

We ask your blessings on the Church and pray that we will always manage this institution consistent with your will.

May the Church open its arms to welcome all people of the world, while not compromising its standards in order to appeal to variant life styles. May there be harmony between the various denominations and within each particular denomination as well. May congregations everywhere be aware that they are all seeking the same goal.

Remove from us feelings of religious bigotry or divisiveness. Above all, let your Church shape the values of society; rather than society shaping the values of the Church.

Prayer for the Armed Forces

Dear God,

Bless and preserve the men and women in our armed forces. May they ever be a deterrent to war without having to fight one.

Help our top level command take measures to make the military life a more wholesome and Christian environment. This life of service should be associated with patriotism and a desire to protect one's fellow citizens, not a playground of drugs, prostitutes, and drunkenness. May basic training emphasize these values.

Bless the chaplains and may their influence be strong and lasting. If our forces must go into battle, may they do so only in defense of our nation, with trust in you and faith in Jesus in their hearts.

Prayer Concerning Luxury

Dear God,

Make our lives less dependent upon luxury. We spend so much money on consumer goods which actually provide only a negligible contribution to our general comfort and satisfaction. Much conspicuous consumption is done simply to gain the admiration and envy of others, and we do pay a price for such status seeking.

Let us realize that we can spend less money on consumer goods and luxuries without denying ourselves any real comfort or happiness. Thus, we'll have more money to contribute to your work in this world.

May we find luxurious living by contributing to the Church, the needy, and projects that make for a better society. This type of expression might even impress others more than an expensive new car.

Prayer Concerning Judgement

Dear God,

Make me less judgmental toward others. It seems so human to criticize and to want to measure others by my own value scale. Yet, I know that these tendencies are really motivated by immaturity, lack of sophistication, and insecurity in my own life.

Help me to be slow in judging others and to try and understand what motivates in them the qualities which I find objectionable. We are all shaped to some degree by forces over which we have no control. Make me aware that there are probably others judging me. Finally, may I remember the Biblical admonition to "Judge not, that ye be not judged."

Prayer Concerning Gossip

Dear God,

Help us to curb our tendencies to gossip about others. It not only violates the Golden Rule, but it is a shameful waste of time and mental energy as well.

Let us raise our minds to higher thought levels than the daily private affairs of another person. There are more important issues with which we should involve ourselves than idle gossip. May we remember why we have minds and voices in the first place. They are too valuable to waste on trivial talk.

Prayer Concerning Our Time

Dear God,

Help me to better use and budget my time. Time is life. One who wastes time is wasting his or her life.

In budgeting my time, may I always remember to allocate first the time I owe to you. Earning enough money to support myself and family should come next, followed by legal and personal obligations. The remaining time for pleasure or recreation can still be used for constructive purposes and self-improvement. Help me apply the old saying, "You can judge people best by observing how they use their leisure time." May my time always be well budgeted, not wasted, and may I stick to the schedule I set for myself.